SUCCESS MADE SIMPLE

Becoming Uncommon in a Common World

Author

Dylon P. Hibbard

Contents

1. Find your why

2. Habits & Goals

3. Master your craft

4. Get Uncomfortable, Stay balanced

5. Embrace your Failures

Take Action!!

Authors Note

I can still feel the chill of that Thursday night and the loose gravel stuck on the bottoms of my bare feet as I walked down the street. I can feel the tears rolling down my face and the absolute emptiness and despair. I was completely broken. It wasn't the first time and it definitely wasn't going to be the last. I was confused, prideful, negative, selfish, and I thought I was 10 feet tall and bullet proof. Nothing could stop me. Life was easy, all I had to do was talk about how successful I was going to be in the future. One day it would just fall into my lap, right? I heard about talking things into existence one time. Sounded easy enough, so when people would ask me what I was going to be. I said "I am going to be a successful businessman with a different car for everyday of the week. A house in Spain, Australia, Colorado, Beverly Hills, and 800 acres of prime land with a log cabin mansion in Alabama." I thought to myself. "Easy right?"

So, on I went talking and talking to anybody who wanted to hear about how I was going to be this super rich guy living the high roller life. The more time that went by the bigger my chest got poked out and the higher I held my head. Until I realized I was full of more crap than a Christmas goose. A couple smacks in the face by life and I fell down quicker than house made of straw. I was stubborn so I kept on trying to speak things into existence without putting in any work whatsoever. I began to find it very odd that these things that I was attempting to speak into existence were not happening for me. A couple of lightbulbs came on in my head every now and then and I told myself "You know what? I think speaking things into existence is only part of this success formula."

We can talk the talk all we want. When it's time for us to actually get tested, that's when we really see the moxie. When your life is turned upside down, that's when you can really see if you can walk the walk. Life is kind of like the weather. It can be the most beautiful, breath taking thing that you have ever experienced, or it can be a dark hurricane with a little earthquake and typhoon on the side. Guess what. No matter what our planet has gone through, an ice age, 2 world wars, pollution, global warming, etc. our mother earth has **adapted and overcame** every last punch in the face. ADAPT and OVERCOME. It sounds so simple, but when its actually time and you have lost everything that you cared for and worked for in your life in the matter of 24 hours. That's when the real test begins. There are only 2 options.

#1 Accept your fate and give up, or

#2 Squeeze every last drop of knowledge out of that learning experience and thrive from it.

Once again it sounds so easy. Only when you are tested do you find out your true colors. So, I began my journey to true success. I Humbled myself and started from scratch reading every book about success that I could put my hands on, watching every video and documentary. The more I studied this the more I wanted it. I slowly began to understand that success is not just a hobby it's a lifestyle. It is not something you can just dabble in every now and then and expect an amazing result. It is a dedication of your life to reaching deep within and finding out how much potential you have and putting it all into play.

After studying absolutely everything I could put my hands on I began to see a pattern amongst all of the fluff. Some people try and make success seem so difficult and use big words and complicated formulas.

Well, I am not the smartest guy in the world, so I took everything I learned and made it as simple as possible and it made it a lot easier to understand. That's what this book is all about. There is no reason to try and hide the simple success formula.

I want to thank everyone who has supported me throughout my life to get me to where I am today.

Pop-
  You have set a great example for me. Your leadership is incredible and inspiring. You have an incredible story and an inspiring one at that. Thank you for

always pushing me to become a better man. You are the greatest man I know.

Mom-

You are the sweetest most caring woman I know. Thank you for always supporting me in whatever I put my mind to. You have never given up on me and always believed in me. I hope that I can find a woman that is sharp as you to become my wife one day.

Jackson-

You have always given me accountability whether you knew that or not. I have always tried to set a great example for you. Thank you for being a great brother.

Taylor-

You push me to become a better man every day and I can't thank you enough for that! You give me something to look forward to and something to chase!

This book is dedicated to my grandmother. She was the sweetest woman ever made. I love you and miss you!

Marjorie Frances Webb

November 15, 1941 – December 17, 2016

Step 1

Find Your Why

Step 1- Write down why you are reading this book.

_____
_____
_____

Step 2- Write down what you want to achieve by reading this book.

_____
_____
_____

Step 3- Write down the timeline you are giving yourself to finish this book.

_____
_____
_____

Step 4- Write down your dream job.

_____
_____
_____

Step 5- Write down your vision for your life 20 years from now.

_____
_____
_____

Step 6- What is your motivation.

_____
_____
_____

Have you grown up wondering why everyone just goes with the flow and you want to break free, but never seem able to muster up the courage? Well, now is the time to take charge of your life and become who you want to be! It's time to quit being a puppet in the game.

Remember when you were a kid and your imagination was just flowing with incredible ideas. You could be anything that you wanted to be. You could go outside with a stick and a couple of friends and conquer the world. What happened to that imagination? Most of you are going to say well I grew up and life just isn't that way. Some of you might vividly remember this. It could have been your parents telling you to "grow up, there is a real world out there and dreamers are losers in the real world." It could have been something that you read. It could have even been one of your friends telling you that it wasn't cool to do that anymore. Did you ask why or just say yea, you are right I am being dumb?

Well I am here to say never stop dreaming about the unthinkable. Never stop using your imagination. It's not just for kids, it is for the uncommon. The world changers and the misfits. Everyone has their reasons for doing what they love. Keep your vision strong and your eyes set on your vision in life and do not quit.

"ALWAYS ASK YOURSELF IF WHAT YOUR'E DOING TODAY IS GETTING

YOU CLOSER TO WHERE YOU WANT TO BE TOMORROW"

What if you never stopped using your imagination and dreaming the way you did as a child? What would be different in your life right now. Would you have a different career. Would you still be married to the same person? We need more people in this world who will ask that simple question. What if?

Think about why you want to be successful and who you want to do it for. It could be just for yourself or it could be for your kids or it could simply be because you were always told that you would never amount to anything. Use that reason **why** to push you through the hard times when you are struggling and believe me times are going to get tough. You are either going to fold under pressure or thrive and push through it because you are focused and determined to hit your goals to reach your vision and be who you want to be.

Q-Do you remember the day that you started to constrict your imagination?

_____

Q-Are you really happy with where you are at in life?

_____

"NEVER GIVE UP, GREAT THINGS TAKE TIME"

There will be many people and things that will hold you back on your path to success. There is more than likely something or someone that is holding you back right now. You are going to have to make the decision to take that thing or person out of your life. Maybe it is someone who has been your childhood friend for many years that keeps getting you to go to the bar when you should really be home mastering your craft. It could be that negative family member who tells you how dumb your ideas are, and you should just give up and quit dreaming because that isn't reality. Maybe that thing that is holding you back is alcohol or drugs or just being plain lazy. This whole book is showing you that you can make one of two decisions in life. Either you can keep doing what is getting you nowhere or you can take massive action and become uncommon amongst a world of common people and change the world. It is time to stand up for yourself and for your future and shed the old and begin the new. Most of the time you don't even have to say anything. The more you focus on becoming successful in whatever you want to do the more those types of people will just fade away. The fact that you even picked this book up means that you are ready for a change and ready to break free from the chains of common and ordinary. You could be the next Mark Zuckerberg, Steve Jobs, Warren Buffet, or simply the first you! Your opportunities can be endless with the right mindset. Of course, not everyone is born into money or has both parents, but if you are using that as your reason on why you aren't successful you are going to need to cut that out immediately. In this chapter your main goal is to find **Your Reason Why**. Do not let fear or embarrassment or anything else get in your way of what you are truly passionate about and what you want to do with your life.

"I WILL NOT FEAR. FEAR IS THE MIND KILLER. FEAR IS THE LITTLE DEATH THAT BRINGS TOTAL OBLITERATION. I WILL FACE MY FEAR. I WILL PERMIT IT TO PASS OVER ME AND THROUGH ME, AND WHEN IT HAS GONE PAST, I WILL TURN THE INNER EYE TO SEE ITS PATH. WHERE THE FEAR HAS GONE

THERE WILL BE NOTHING, ONLY I REMAIN"

- Frank Herbert

With that being said, whatever your passion is in life pursue that with massive action. Do not ever let someone tell you that your dream is impossible. Embrace fear and failure with extreme passion. Do what others are afraid to do and unleash the power from within yourself. When others ask you why you succeed and they don't, tell them this:

"I succeed because I am willing to do the things you are not. I will fight against the odds. I will sacrifice. I am not shackled by fear, insecurity or doubt. I feel those emotions, but I drink them in and then swallow them away to the blackness of hell. I am motivated by accomplishment, not pride. Pride consumes the weak and kills their heart from within. If I fall... I will get up. If I am beaten... I will return. I will

never stop getting better. I will never give up… EVER. That is why I succeed."

- Tony Evans

Commit this quote to memory every day. Put it on your bathroom mirror or in your car or save it as your home screen on your phone. Once you hear yourself say this enough, you are going to start to believe it and that along with massive action and discipline on your life you will be unstoppable.

Always know that you are incredibly special. It doesn't matter the color of your skin, your religious preference, your sexual orientation or your age. We were all put on this earth for a reason and it wasn't to wake up, waste time and die. We are meant to live incredible lives! It is time to start molding yourself into the person you were meant to become. It is time for you to break free of the daily vertigo and completely break yourself down into nothing and rebuild.

CHALLENGE # 1

- Go over the questions at the beginning of this chapter. Take 20 minutes out of your day and put your phone on silent and lock the door and think about what you truly want to do with your life. **FIND YOUR WHY!** Create yourself a life motto that you are going to live by and commit it to memory within a week. For example, here is mine when I first began my journey:

"I want to succeed as bad as I want to breathe, I want to succeed more than I want to sleep. Day by day until my last breath. I will never quit. I will never stop getting better. I will be the motivator. I will set the example, raise the bar, and beat the odds. I will leave a true legacy behind. I will show you how great I am."

MY NEW LIFE MOTTO

_____

_____

_____

_____

Notes

Step 2

Habits & Goals

Step 1- Write down your bad habits.

_____

_____

_____

_____

_____

_____

Step 2- Write down why you started those bad habits.

_____

_____

_____

Step 3- Write down your good habits.

_____

_____

_____

_____

_____

_____

Step 4- What is the first bad habit you want to get rid of?

_____

_____

_____

I trust that you have found your reason why you want to break out of the common world and make a name for yourself. Now that we have that goal for our life, it's time to clean house on our old boring life. In this chapter we will discuss the importance of instilling good habits in our lives as soon as possible. Think of the good habits as our solid foundation for our new life so we can be prepared for all of the blows we are going to take along the journey. There are going to be more failures than you can even imagine, but with the right foundation and our eyes on target we can be **Unstoppable!**

GOOD HABITS

Building good habits in your life is like setting a solid foundation before your build your house. After you have found your motivation and your reason why you want to be successful (*step 1*), it's time to start building your solid foundation. Imagine that you are demolishing your current house to build a newer and improved one because it has a terrible mold in it that has started to spread. If you don't destroy it the mold will spread throughout the entire house and you will lose everything. So, we are going to salvage what we can and destroy everything else. The sooner you do this the more you can save from your house.

Let's start by saving all of our good habits and get simple with it. Look at your list of good habits, now add the simple ones like brushing your teeth every day. Well I really hope that is one of your simple ones. Let them add up. Now remember this is all you have to start your new life. You should be extremely proud of every good habit that you have instilled in yourself over your life time.

A good habit is a behavior that is beneficial to one's physical or mental health, often linked to a high level of discipline and self-control.

When you are looking at your good habit list and it is not beneficial to your physical or mental health, take it off. When you are looking for new good habits to build your new successful life on, always refer back to this. We are trying to make this as simple as possible. The best and one of the simplest new good habits to start every day is to make your bed when you wake up. Just set a goal to make your bed every day for a week. You will soon start to feel pride in making your bed and eventually it will become part of your lifestyle where your body has to do it, or you feel weird and lazy.

Starting these good habits off small is key. Think of it as the snowball effect. The small good habits start getting bigger the more time you give to roll. It is going to make the bigger tasks a lot easier when you get to them.

"EVERYTHING IN MODERATION, EVEN MODERATION"

Building good habits takes extreme amounts of discipline and self-control. You will fail at this too but remember that every time you fail you are getting closer to success.

5 pillars of developing good habits

Discipline

Self-control

Patience

Persistence

Consistency

These five pillars are crucial to your early success in creating good habits. Just like the pillars that hold up a house you will need all of them for it to be stable. If you only use just a few, your house will eventually fall. Going through the motions on your path to becoming successful will ultimately end up in failure until you quit and settle with being common for the rest of your life. These five pillars aren't just used in creating a stable platform for your future habits, they can be applied to everything in life. That's why starting with this is key.

1. **<u>Discipline</u>**

This is key in everyday life and one of the most important cornerstones to a successful life. Without discipline it will be easier to become lazy and forget about your goals that you have set for your life. You will just "get to them later" or "start tomorrow". You must develop this good habit first and as soon as possible.

2. **Self- Control**

   The ability to withstand temptation. Whether that be with things or people, we all have that one thing or person that we should indulge in but sometimes we do anyway. With self-control we will be able to withstand the temptations of falling off of the path. This will keep our minds focused on the goal at hand with a barrier to shield distractions.

3. **Patience**

In today's world we have a short attention span. We expect everything right then and we get upset when we don't get what we want in a short period of time. That is why there are very few uncommon people in todays world. Those people have mastered the good habit of patience. You are going to have to be willing to put in years of work to become successful not hours. Remember the saying that it takes 10,000 hours to become a pro.

So, until you have hit that amount of time keep your head down and press.

4. **Persistence**

You must push through the storm when it comes. Do not let failing at your goal a couple of times deter you from pushing forward. If anything, it should drive you to achieve your goal even more. Always keep pushing to make yourself better and always keep pushing for that vision that you have in life.

5. **Consistency**

The last of the five pillars and not the least is consistency. Once you build up your good habits, the goal is to keep them. That means every single day to consistently keep these good habits in your life. It only takes a couple of days to throw your whole process of track.

Bad Habits

What comes to mind when you think of bad habits? A bad habit is anything that has a bad effect on you that you repeatedly do. The main points could be on your mind, body, finances, and relationships. Now think about what bad habits that you have that could be affecting you in the wrong manner. Now write them down.

_____

_____

Now that you have these on paper, write beside them how they affect you and in what category they would be in. They could be in one or all four. Your bad habits will never disappear completely, but we can put new good habits in their place. For every bad habit, you will need a good one to put in its place. Here is an example. Fill in the empty spaces.

BAD HABIT	**GOOD HABIT**
Now I…	Instead I will…

Smoke	Chew gum
Eat fast food	Cook my food
Waste time when I get home from work	Go to the gym

Goals

Without a target you have nothing to hit

Goal setting is key in the success and failure of any individual. You are walking blind on your path to become a legend without goals. So how do goals work and why should I use them?

A goal is simply a target you set for yourself in the near or distant future with the intention on hitting it by putting forth effort. Simple right? Then why do people make it seem so hard. There is a million and one reasons why hitting goals are hard. People are afraid of one big thing, FAILURE. We will talk about FEAR and FAILURE later on, but for now let's just keep it at that. Goals are meant to be hit. Goals are not all supposed to be some extravagant outlandish thing. They vary from all different sizes to setting a goal to make your bed every day for a week to make a million dollars by the time you are 30. Once we learn how to use goals to its highest capacity, then we will increase our success on becoming legends. How many people do you know that have big goals in life? Maybe a lot, most likely not many. If you ask all the people that you know what their monthly goals are, they would probably look at you a little funny or just make up some random stuff to make it look like they are on top of their game. One of the keys in becoming uncommon in a common world is setting yourself apart with the little things. You are going to meet many people who fake their way through life and lie about being successful. They will buy cars and houses that they can't afford and make it look like on the outside that they are successful. Just give it a couple of years, they will be up to their eyeballs in debt and move back in with their parents.

3 S's of Goal setting

Start small

Stay consistent

See it through

Just like we learn to master our craft we must master other things along with it and one of those very important tools to master is goals. **Starting small** in goal setting is crucial. You want to see success immediately. You want to show yourself that it is possible to hit that target. Once you hit that first goal there is a sense of self-empowerment within you. Next step is to set another one and then another one after that. **Staying consistent** builds a firm foundation in your mind and it gets stronger and stronger each time you set and hit another goal. Even when this gets monotonous, **See it through**. You never know what you will learn and experience by doing this.

You will more than likely start very strong on your goals. You will hit that first one fairly quick and you will feel unstoppable. Eventually the dopamine feeling that comes with accomplishing a goal starts to fade and you start to relax, and each goal gets bigger and bigger. At this point refer back to the ***3 S's of goal setting*** and set a small goal to get the ball rolling again.

"Excellence Has No Finish Line"

Never quit on yourself after the first lap. Setting goals and hitting them should become a habit that you don't even have to think about doing. Because goals are just a small part of your vision in life.

Write down a goal that you are going to hit within a week.

_____
_____
_____

Now, write the date that you are going to accomplish this.

_____

Notes

Step 3

Master Your Craft

Everyone has greatness within

Q- What is your passion?

_____

_____

_____

_____

_____

Q- Are you doing everything in your power to master it? Circle YES or NO

Q- Are you willing to put yourself in uncomfortable situations in order to instill the discipline you will need in your life to become successful? Circle YES or NO

When we grow up, we experiment with different hobbies and interests until we find that AHA moment when we really get interested in a certain field of study. Some of us are still looking for that interesting hobby today. It's an incredible feeling when we find it. I know for me when I find something new that I'm really interested in I can't get enough of it. I want to know everything about it. For some people with an entrepreneurial mindset, they are usually looking at new ways to make money on the side. Some search for the next big thing, while others just search for that niche to hustle on the weekend for some extra cash. Don't get too caught up in searching for what your "calling" is or what you are passionate about. Just relax. You have already probably found it and either don't think that you can monetize it or you are probably ten plus years in your career that you chose for yourself and are too afraid to take that leap of faith to make your passion your full time job.

When you become a master of your craft whatever it is, you set yourself apart from the common people. You turn yourself into a polished turd in laymen's terms. This takes absolute ***dedication*** and ***persistence***. I know that you have probably heard the saying that *"If you* *love what you do, you will never work a day in your life"*. When you are truly passionate about what you do and you are proud to call it your job, you will automatically put more effort into it. When you are at a 9-5 job that you hate but you don't see any way of getting out of it because you have a family to feed and bills to pay it's a little harder to put that same effort into it.

You have a simple decision to make when you are stuck in this situation.

1. **EASY ROUTE.**

    You can accept your fate and hate your job for the next 20-30 years of your life, while you watch others live out their dream because they chose to sacrifice while you sat on the couch and watched Netflix and complained about your job.

2. **HARD ROUTE.**

You can do everything in your power to get yourself out of that situation. Work from 9am-5pm then come home and eat dinner and spend time with the kids and from 10pm-2am you do what you have to do to master your craft that you actually care about and that you are passionate about. You still get six hours of sleep at night and that's 4 hours every night during the week and probably more during the weekend to make your dream a reality. Let's just say that it's just 4 hours every night that you put into your dream that you were probably spending on your phone or watching pointless stuff on Netflix. That is **1,460** hours in a year that you can spend productively. That is **2 months** out of the year spent grinding on your passion becoming a true legend! Just 4 hours a day. All it comes down to is work ethic. Are you actually going to put the work in? Or are you going to give up after a couple of days? And worst of all **are you just going to talk about it and not be about it?**

True legends are made in the face of adversity. Buckle down and master your craft. Bring together a little passion and a lot of work ethic and make your dreams become a reality. For those of you that played sports, that extra set or that extra rep everyday pays off during game time when you have more practice and training than your opponent. Whether you like it or not this is a battle to the top. I don't know about you, but I want to be at the top!

Get Off Your Phone

Our phones are most likely within a hands reach at all times of the day. A person spends an average of 4 hours on their phone every day. That is the same amount of time that we talked about mastering your craft. Well when you say you don't have time, think again. **YOU ARE WASTING AWAY TWO MONTHS A YEAR OF YOUR LIFE!** There it is, be honest with yourself. Are you truly trying to be productive when you open up Facebook, Instagram, Snap Chat, Twitter, and all of those other apps? I ask that question because you can use those platforms to make some great connections to build your brand or your business. Our phones are one of the greatest procrastination tools of this generation. It is so easy to take yourself out of an awkward situation by getting on your phone. The next time to go to the doctor and you are sitting in the waiting room, take a look around. everyone is on their phones. With the benefit of the doubt given maybe 1 of them are actually putting work in. I honestly believe that social media is the drug of choice in today's world. It can drive people to fame or death.

Everyone has greatness within them! Once you have started to master your craft, start to build your Mastermind Group together. Imagine a conference room with nine chairs and you are at the head of the table. Who would you have in those chairs if you could pick anyone in the world in the present, past, or future to be there to help you achieve your dream?

MY DREAM TEAM

1. _____
2. _____
3. _____
4. _____
5. _____
6. _____
7. _____
8. _____
9. _____

You are not going to be able to achieve your dreams by yourself no matter how talented or wise that you think you are. You have to have a team behind you. Now that you have your dream team picked out, learn from them and soak in all of their wisdom like a **SPONGE!**

CHALLENGE #3

- Intentionally think about whether you are wasting time or being productive

when you are on your phone throughout the day.
- Try spending just an hour every day working toward your passion with no distractions. If you can manage that keep upping the time until you have proper balance.
- After you figure our who is going to be on your dream team, keep the roster somewhere where you can reference it like on your desk or in your wallet.

Notes

Step 4

Get Uncomfortable, Stay Balanced

We are in a world of "common is comfortable" and "I don't want to stand out". The misfits are the people who actually change the world. Going against the flow and standing firm in your beliefs and keeping your eyes on your vision in life is key in becoming successful in today's world. With your new habits built and your foundation on solid ground it's time to step it up to another level. You can have the fastest car in the world but if you don't use it to its fullest potential. Why even have it at all? You really want to spend that much money on it for the looks and to just cruise around in it. Absolutely not. It is the same concept with building yourself into whoever you want to become. Are you going to spend years and years of your life rebuilding and fine tuning your mind, body and lifestyle just to do nothing with it? Well that is what is going to happen if you are afraid to be different.

Step out of your comfort zone. Learn A new Hobby. Study a new language. Meet new people. If you really want to become successful you are going to have to push yourself to new limits every day for the rest of your life. You should never go a day without setting a goal and hitting it. You should never go a week without looking back on it to learn from your mistakes you should never go a year without hitting at least **12** goals. There is never going to be a time where you hit a goal and say I did it. I hit my goal now

I'm done, now I'm going to go back to blending in and accepting average. This is going to become an addiction! So, get ready for the ride.

You can have all of the right habits in place and the right mindset and the right goals with the perfect vision in life and run around in circles chasing your tail if you don't have the right **Balance** in your life. Since I have been on this journey to find my fullest potential, I have discovered just that, and I would get upset with myself and wonder what I was doing wrong. Our journey in life to reach our vision and become successful is a never-ending puzzle. We are constantly adding pieces and trying new and different ones until the piece fits. We can only fit one piece at a time even though sometimes we want to put the whole puzzle together in one night.

I picked three categories that I knew that if I kept balanced, I could stay on track and stay at top speed through my day and my life. I picked these three things and added to them as needed. Now these three categories might be different for yourself. ***MIND, BODY, FINANCES***.

MIND

Every day I try and stimulate my mind instead of becoming a zombie scrolling through social media. Here are some examples:

- Read
- Meditate
- Pray
- Vision yourself achieving your next goal

BODY

You only have one body, so you need to treat it as such. Take care of it and keep it at top shape as much as possible. You will thank yourself years down the road. Here are some examples:
- Go to the gym
- Go for a run
- Eat healthy
- Hydrate properly
- Watch the amount of alcohol going into your body

FINANCES

Now that your mind and your body are stimulated throughout the day. Take care of your finances. It doesn't matter if you are making 30 thousand dollars a year or 500 thousand. If you spend more than you make you will be putting yourself in a hole. Money problems is one of the leading causes of divorce and suicide. Its really not that hard. Live within your means and be patient. Don't go and buy a car that you can just make the payments on. Go ahead and save up for it and pay cash. Some people will never get out of debt just because they want to appear as if they are living the rich and famous lifestyle

when their bank account says otherwise. Here are some examples:
- Budget out each paycheck
- Stop eating out so much
- Start paying cash for things
- Start a $1000 emergency fund

Life is just a game. There are winners and losers and there always will be. What are you going to do differently to become a winner?

_____

_____

_____

_____

_____

_____

_____

_____

_____

CHALLENGE #4

- What three categories are you going to use as a cornerstone to a balanced life?

    1._____
    2._____
    3._____

- What thing are you going to do this week to put you out of your comfort zone?

    _____

    _____

    _____

    _____

    _____

- Pick three people who are in your life right now or who have passed who are important to you in this journey to success.

    1._____

    2._____

    3._____

Notes

Step 5

Embrace Your Failures

Records are meant to be broken

Where there is a will there is a way. There are so many success stories of people coming from absolutely terrible circumstances and turning coal into a Dimond. Here are a few words of encouragement from some very successful people for example:

"I had failed on an epic scale. An exceptionally short-lived marriage had imploded, and I was jobless, a lone parent, and as poor as it is possible to be in modern Britain, without being homeless. The fears that my parents had had for me, and that I had had for myself, had both come to pass, and by every usual standard, I was the biggest failure I knew."

- J.K. Rowling

"I didn't see it then, but it turned out that getting fired from Apple was the best thing that could have ever happened to me."

- Steve Jobs

"Success is failure in progress."

-Albert Einstein

"My great concern is not whether you have failed, but whether you are content with your failure."

— Abraham Lincoln

"I've missed more than 9000 shots in my career. I've lost almost 300 games. 26 times, I've been trusted to take the game winning shot and missed. I've failed over and over and over again in my life. And that is why I succeed."

-Michael Jordan

"Even though I get older, what I do never gets old, and that's what I think keeps me hungry."

- Steven Spielberg

"We don't look backwards for very long. We keep moving forward, opening up new doors, and doing new things, because we're curious… and curiosity keeps leading us down new paths."

- Walt Disney

"If you hear a voice within you say, 'you cannot paint,' then by all means paint, and that voice will be silenced."

- Vincent Van Gogh

These people are no greater than you. They found their reason why and they stuck with it no matter what. They let their failures become teaching tools instead of piercing heavy stones. These are just a few of your uncommon people in our common world. They are going to leave a legacy just because they made a decision to pursue their passion and vision in life no matter what got thrown at them. The failures don't get easier, they more often than not get harder and harder.

But they will always make your stronger on the other side

"LET YOUR SCARS REMIND YOU OF HOW STRONG YOU REALLY ARE"

Q- What do you fear?

_____

_____

Most people fear failure. To become successful, you must embrace failure. It will be the best teaching tool of your life. Swallow your pride and actually act on those crazy ideas and don't worry on whether they will work or not the first time or the 100th time. Just know that you will take each failure as a learning experience and one step closer to the final product. One day you are going to achieve what you put your mind to. One of the only differences between a successful person and a common person is the common person gave up. They could have been one idea away from greatness. There could have been so close they could have touched it and didn't even know, but they quit. and that is the ultimate difference between a winner and a loser. The winner will never give up and will always keep pushing forward until they have reached their goal.

Distractions and bumps in the road are inevitable. Don't get mad at yourself for falling off track for a little while. You aren't perfect and you never will be. It takes extreme courage to step back into the battlefield of life to stay at it day in and day out. You aren't going to hit all of your goals in a year and then sit back and live the easy life for the rest of your days on earth. You are going to have to become addicted to the game of life. Love every part of it! The preparation and the planning and when its game time, you will be able to attack with everything you have!

Think about your life as a famer. Spend every waking moment preparing your fields for rain and when it comes, whenever that day is you are ready for it! If you embrace the journey of life and are grateful for each day you have you are going to have one hell of a good life!

Don't think that having a lot of money and a lot of success in your life is going to make you happy. Don't think that giving yourself a break on the weekends and living for Friday night is going to give you happiness. Don't think for a single second that finding the end of that bottle or the end of that joint is going to give you happiness. Maybe all of those things might give you short term happiness, but not long-term and whoever tells you otherwise is lying to you. To become a true legend in today's world you are going to have to know upfront that you have to be happy with yourself and confident in yourself and no short-term success or numb will keep you happy. You have to be comfortable in your own shoes and know your fullest potential is within yourself.

Stop trying to find gratification in other people because at the end of the day you are the one who is making the decision to become a legend and you are the one who is putting in the work while other people are playing. You should be proud of that! Also know that ***actions speak way louder than words*** and the people who need to know your plans will, period. There is no need to tell every person that gives you a second that you are putting in the work to become a millionaire or start your own business or to play professional sports etc. Let your hard work and dedication speak for you and trust me, once other people notice that you have your mind set on your vision in life, they will do the talking for you.

You will not be remembered for how many times you have failed in life, you will be remembered for that one time that you broke the seal and discovered a whole new gear that you didn't know you had and achieved something great! All of that hard work and dedication will pay off one day only if you never give up on your goals in life. NEVER, NEVER, NEVER, NEVER, NEVER, NEVER, NEVER GIVE UP!!!

CHALLENGE #5

- Find something that you have given up on because you could never seem to get it write and start that flam e back up just to prove to yourself that you will not give up until you have achieved your goal. What is that?

_____

_____

_____

- Find three distractions that are in your way right now and work on cutting them out of your life. What are they?

    1._____

    _____

    2._____

    _____

    3._____

    _____

- Work on just putting work in and grinding instead of telling others your plans.

Notes

Take Action!!

As I come to a close in this book, I hope that you have collected a couple of forward-thinking habits along with a solid foundation on a successful lifestyle. Just because this is the end of the book doesn't mean it is the end of yours, so with that being said this last chapter is yours. Take charge of it just like you are taking charge of your life. Be creative.

Be powerful. Be courageous. You are amazing and it is now time for you to start building your legacy for generations to come.

Remember that the amount of input equals the amount of output. When you find what you are passionate about and what you want to build your legacy around, dive in head first and put your entire soul into it. The world is at your fingertips! Write this last chapter and feel free to email it to me. I would love to see your plan for your life!

MY CHAPTER

_____

_____

www.ingramcontent.com/pod-product-compliance
Lightning Source LLC
Chambersburg PA
CBHW022010170526
45157CB00003B/1214